dyingful

akhira

dyingful

Copyright © 2023 by akhira

independently published

ISBN: 9798395910974

instagram.com/dyingful
instagram.com/akhirapoetry
twitter.com/akhirapoetry
tiktok.com/@akhirapoetry

the explanation

"dyingful"
a collection of poems
i have been writing since i was 17
my heart was broken
i put all my pain and love into this
i love you
thank you for reading
enjoy

the wolf in sheep skin

nowhere to run
nowhere to hide
can't find
what i'm looking for

if you leave with me now
we both might get what we want

destruction in her absence
won't bring comfort in my heart

she chose a path without me
and i chose loss over god

got what we desired
lost my soul in the fire
the relief wasn't worthwhile

i was the sheep
and she was wolf in sheep skin

confused

i'm sad again but i have to carry on
like nothing's wrong

i'm fucking confused
how i fall out of love
with everything new

alone and it's comforting
depressed and i'm suffering
my passion won't last long

i'm sad again but i have to carry on
like nothing's wrong

maybe if i fall in love with my depression
it will leave me too

akhira

you're always there
somewhere in my mind

i broke my own heart trying to be enough for you

akhira

i loved you and sometimes you loved me too

it hurts me every time i'm missing you

one day i hope you understand
how much you meant to me

i should have trusted my trust issues

akhira

and suddenly we were strangers again

i lost myself while trying not to lose you

we were never meant to be
but i always wanted us to be

dyingful

what if we fell in love at the wrong time?

akhira

i know you are somewhere
with someone else and it hurts

i miss you, the old you,
the one who used to care about me

losing my friends broke my heart too

i try not to think because whenever i do,
i become discontent with everything i do

akhira

i forgive you but i don't trust you anymore

after all that we had, we act like
we had never met

i loved you so much
that even when
you hurt me
i tried to understand you

i miss you all the time
but i never tell you

akhira

i knew i loved you
when i couldn't
hate you
for breaking my heart

i think we were meant to be
but we did it wrong

why am i waiting for someone
who doesn't give a fuck about me?

nobody cares unless you're beautiful or dead

i'm letting you go so i can start again

i can't trust anyone but i trusted you

i hope you miss me sometimes

i miss how you wanted me

akhira

don't worry, the right one won't leave

dyingful

you destroyed me and i apologized

i'm gonna be happy one day
and it's gonna be for me

i don't want to spend my whole life
trying to get over you

we went through all that
just to be strangers again

i don't know what hurts more,
missing you or pretending not to

akhira

someday someone will love you
and you will forget
why no one else never could

hurt before so i don't care anymore

you're losing interest in me
and i fucking hate
i can feel the love between us fading
but i will love you unconditionally
even if it's not me with you

please stay
until i have fallen out of love with you
so it won't hurt bad
when you leave

akhira

i knew she was hurting
by the way she was texting

i started to leave before anyone could leave me

not everyone you lose is a loss

you are you and that's enough

i hope you become happier

i can see you are tired
i can see you are sad

you don't wanna talk
rather sleep the pain away

exhausted from work
been a long time
since you have seen
happy days

and i cry about it
cry about it
sometimes
i just want you to be fine

that's been my only wish
for a very long time

and i cry about it
cry about it
sometimes

i fucking loved you, why wasn't that enough?

akhira

the love you give will come back to you soon

i try not to miss you, i try to let go
but in the end, you're always on my mind

akhira

i still love you but you don't care

i miss you but you seem fine without me

akhira

maybe i'm just hard to love
and easy to leave

because no matter what i'd still choose you

i don't wanna let it go because i still love you

we are not close anymore
but i will be here if you need me

akhira

i will not be your second choice
not when you've always been my first

i'm trying to forget you
but i'm also waiting for you to come back

i lost myself in you and then i lost you

maybe you're someone else's meant to be

i still care about you, i'm just tired

i wanted you so much,
i didn't even care
if it was toxic or not

akhira

please be patient with me,
i'm working on loving myself

and just like that, i lost you

i will wish for you one last time

i will never stop loving you
even if we're not together

i showed you all of me too soon

you just looked at those messages
i sent and left me on read

i want someone who sees the bad
in me and still wants to stay

dyingful

maybe i loved you too much too soon

akhira

one day you will realize how much i cared

i broke my own heart
because i expected too much

akhira

and we didn't talk after that

i ruined what we had because i was sad

akhira

you broke me but i still wait for you

dyingful

choose someone who chooses you

akhira

i let you in and you completely destroyed me

i miss the way i felt when i first met you

akhira

i really do miss what we almost had

i know what's inside of me
was never enough

akhira

i get jealous because i don't want to lose you

dyingful

i'm letting go because i need to grow

i wish that i was what you wanted

dyingful

i miss how me and you used to be

akhira

at night i kind of just scroll through instagram,
listen to music and think about you

dyingful

how can i love you, when
i can't even love myself

akhira

i fucking miss you but i can't tell you that

don't treat the right person wrong

akhira

i'm sorry i wasn't everything you ever wanted

you gave up on us and i never did

akhira

sometimes i still hope,
you will wake up one day and miss me

dyingful

i'm trying to let you go,
but i'm praying you will come back

akhira

i acted like it wasn't a big deal
when really you broke my heart

teeth

losing myself in you
put me through every emotion
maybe you thought about us
maybe you thought about love

hurt before so i don't give a fuck
you kiss me
and pretend this is love

i know i'm not enough
i know you want more

i don't want anyone else
i wanted you to be the one

i'm sad

hate me, hurt me, break me
i'd never leave

fuck me, love me, trust me
i won't ever feel

no matter what I do
she always puts me in a bad mood
she's sad and I'm sad too

can't forget her embrace
keeping me together
when i was falling apart
and she was falling in love

ghoul

when you left
i didn't lose you all at once
i lost you in pieces over time
until all our memories faded
and i didn't want to remember them
without you here with me
it's like we never did anything
all… just to be strangers again
the girl you were,
is now just a memory

the heartbreak that never ends

losing feelings
they all fade
where was i
when you were with him

obsession
with your attention
left me in
broken pieces

couldn't satisfy what I needed
it so happens to be you

temptations
i can't control

wanted you the world and you

destroying myself to get it
cause i never loved myself to begin with

wanted you to love me
even if it meant losing myself to get it

wednesday

the fall
descend
from what was good

now i'm sad and
discontent

my energy changed
bad frequencies comforting me

the desire to inspire my soul never ends
and I keep chasing it

these days i wanna quit
but i can never quit from what saved me

!

because when it's night
all love is gone
and the happy days are no more
i want you to find comfort in me,
when it matters the most

YOU ARE NOT ALONE!

i need a hug right now
stuck in a place
where feelings aren't allowed

remember we were kids
running through the city
no matter the weather

i feel so alone right now
stuck in a place
where no one'es around

hanging out with my friends
i wanna feel that again

10 pm skating through the late night
i wanna feel that again
i wanna feel that again

won't find comfort in crowd
the silence is getting loud
sitting alone in my bed
with the good memories starting to fade
it's all in my head

?

the sadness never ends
you just die from it
and life goes on
without me in it

∞

you loving me won't comfort me
i don't need temporary feelings
if it's not forever
it's whatever

if you gave it time
it would work out fine
need feelings now
feelings fade

you don't love me
the way you used to
it's not bringing me comfort
the way it used to

blocking them is the best closure you can get

not a paragraph
not on good terms
not being reachable
not staying friends
not knowing why
they did what they did

block them

-   *fuck you, next*

cover up
my tears
in words
it's never enough
you don't give a fuck
i was born with hell in my heart

akhira

don't be afraid to let go of your leaves
there is no burden in attachment, grow

I WON'T BREAK...

i'm trying to find
a place outside my mind
where i will feel safe

can't hide behind
i'm just fine
i need change

war inside my head
i won't ever win
i won't ever break

when will it end?

it was 2 am
and we were sitting outside in silence
i was crying
thinking about a past
i'm trying to forget
while you were inside your head
thinking about a future
without me in it
i got issues i don't discuss
without you
i disgust myself
i need help
talking about it doesn't even help
wish i had friends who could help
but i don't even got myself
i know being with me is hell

i will always love you

i love you and i let you go
you hurt me and i let it go
it hurts not texting you back
but i need to move on

missed me when i started to grow
i love her and she loved me too
but it was toxic

my intentions for you were always pure
insecure but of you, i was always fucking sure

i will always love you
but i need to let you go
hurts not to answer your calls
but this time i need to move on

i will always love you
even if i move on

akhira

fuck you, next

i walked her home, for the last time

afraid of endings
i fucked up
our goodbye
didn't want this to end

maybe i'm not enough
and i can't accept it
clairvoyant, always
knew it would come to this

thought i was all of this
while i was none of it
hyping myself up
cause all I had was love for this

your love for me
ran out a long time ago
and every good thing
always fade slow

i didn't want you to go

2017

take me away
from the path
of my broken dreams
you don't believe in

i still want this
more than before
i'm just tired
can never take a break

afraid you will
leave forever and i
won't ever feel the same
with the absence

it's gonna leave
when it's all dead and gone
i want it
to last a little longer

but i guess
things will never be the same
to some people
i am already only a memory

and

don't put me first
like i did
i'm sorry
if what I write

is not enough
for you to stay
i hope you
find that love

somewhere else
i lost myself
chasing this
i'm sorry i wasted
what i was given

the end is nigh

terrified of what we could have been
got tired of fighting for us
i never evolved through pain
how, how they lied to us

and my voice changed
still writing the same
scream more, talk less
can't become my own home

i'm tired
i'm tired
i'm tired of these words
never working out
thought i would've made it by now
i lost my mind
last time
i gave all my time for this

heart hanging on a string
you just played with my feelings
used me, to get over your heartbreak
well now i'm breaking apart

and the words i said
when i should have said nothing

the love that never ends

sometimes i love you
sometimes i hate you
but there isn't one day
that goes by that
i don't miss you

akhira

tired

losing myself in desires
can't fill the void in my chest
emptiness on emptiness
i can't take this

what is happiness?
i find it in words i express
and love i never get
you already have it

i'm losing myself to get it...
is it even worth it in the end

i fill the void in my heart
with attention instead of love

you made me feel like
i needed the whole world to love me
to replace the love
you gave me

sanctuary

there is new a life ahead
a place my fears will disappear

without you
i'll find the light

and do good
with what's left of me

tears i can't wipe

looking for my sanctuary
i won't find

heart eyes

you smile
i smile
we cool
we cool for now

look what you made me become
i'm not the same when i'm in love

heart eyes
heart eyes
i couldn't believe it
you were the only reason
i hanged on

every september

i need a lot reassurance
consumed by my insecurities
growth not found in comfort
i need ease

i need peace
i need my pieces
coming back together
bandaid words
won't fix my heart hurting

akhira

love myself ~ hate myself

i spent this entire year
trying to get over you

too in love
to be anything else

i lost her
i lost a friend

lost love
now i'm trying to love myself
with the broken pieces
you left

she said
"don't say you love me
when you can't even love yourself
don't say you want me
when you don't even know
what you want for yourself"

and i know the love i give
will come back to me soon
and all i wanted was you

heartbreaks and headaches

i'm tired of this
insecure and unstable
i know you don't want none of this

i broke my own heart over it
i can be enough too...
and if you gave me time
maybe i could be what you need too...

but i know...
it's already too late

she don't feel the same
she's in love with someone else

to her
i'm just another end

ocean

drown my feelings out
in tears i hide again

you could see i wasn't okay
there is still fear in my mistakes

i'm insecure of the past
hoping these feelings last

left before i could ask
if what we promised still carry on

you were the reason
i didn't give up

please don't give up on me now
give me time
and i will be enough...

and again

you could mend my heart
if you really wanted to

and i bend your love
to mean what i want it to

i knew it would end too soon...

now all that i remember
is how you used me
and i let you
because i was falling for you

while it lasted...

you can leave if you really want to
it has already happened before
so if you do, i know you had to

put yourself first
cause the world hurt
you too much, girl

i know these days
it's harder to trust
easier to love
easier to get bored

so you can leave
i know that you have to...

can't let go, i'm too in love

i was just another one
to me you were the one

don't say you want to be friends
i know this is all pretend

who hurt you
that made you hurt me

how long?

i know things will never be the same
i can't let go, i'm too in love

in my feelings again
can't handle these feelings again
she really meant everything...
to her i'm just another end...

akhira

wtf i'm crying

you left
like i was never
a reason to stay

akhira

i still remember our last eye contact

dyingful

i didn't say
"i love you"
to hear it back
i said it to make
sure you knew

not the best year, but at least i met you

if it's meant to be
you will come back to me

it's selfish of me
to tell you stay
if you wanna leave

i'm sorry that i'm sorry

with you i lost
all my feelings again
hit a peak
now i can't feel anything

and i search for you
in the time i wasted

what am i so afraid of?

i know i won't ever be enough
and i know
i say sorry too much
and i'm so insecure
with what i want

i'm afraid i will fall the same
... and i will never change
all because you left
i miss you, i'm sorry

wednesday pt. 2

can't seem to forget the pain
she showed

i don't even know what to write
stuck
and
i'm not what you want

and it hurts too much
and the sunshine
she took away
with her bright eyes

i can't look away
all i remember is that fucking wednesday

even though it hurts to say
and i know you don't feel the same

made your words mean what i wanted to
cause i wanted you

and now i miss you more than i should
and i care more than you do
hesitant to tell you
cause i don't wanna lose you

wednesday pt. 3

lost myself
lost you
nobody can help
3 weeks and all i think about is...
how this didn't work out...

maybe if i gave it time
it would have...

but i'm too consumed by my thoughts
of you
and it's too much
to let it go at once

now i'm losing pieces of myself
i won't ever get back

i want you more than any blue sky
i don't care if it rains, cause you're my sunshine

september 25th

i won't pretend it was something
when it was nothing
meant nothing
to you

i been so alone
i been so alone
without you

i have trapped all my love
inside my heart
that always breaks

you won't find
what you want
in me

train wreck of emotions

can't maintain
what good is left
of me

gave my heart
to her
i'm left in pieces

i don't want it back
i have no worth

silence in my chest
i need sleep to escape
my mind
where hell reside

run
run away

from love
every time it enters my heart

but this time i wanted you to stay
even if it hurts
i was willing to wait
for you until the very end

we are not that close

i know
you are tired and bored

i am too
we don't really talk anymore

but i want to
we are not that close

so i stop myself from reaching out to you
annoyed by my presence

i will leave...
so please...
tell me to go...
so i can let go...

whatever of her
i have left in my heart
i can't let go
forever in my mind
i was lost
in love

i don't wanna let it go

distant
you're not listening
and i'm pretending
it does not hurt

you thought i could let it go
but i don't

akhira

in between love and heartbreak

can't get you out of my head
can't get out of bed
i'm stuck
in between love and heartbreak

dyingful

i don't wanna do this anymore

i know you don't wanna
don't wanna
be here, be here
with me

bored with everything
attached, cause i was depressed
ever since september
i haven't been okay

for so long i'm so lost

fucked it all up in a wednesday
can't say
i didn't say
what i wanted to say

you don't wanna stay
you don't
wanna
be here with me

i wasn't worth it
i'm never worth it

my desire was poison
her absence
was my destruction

blood in the sink

and i did what i did
to silence my chest

to rid the thoughts of you in my head
i'm numb again

all progress lost
with the pain gone

i don't wanna be here anymore

make believe

25th to the 10th
i can never change that

made believe
i was worth it

you didn't love me enough to stay
and i love you too much to leave

even if we weren't meant to be
i still wanted to try and make believe
these feelings could have lasted forever

fall frozen leaves
in love with what i can't keep

before i love

show me
i can trust you
show me
you're not gonna break my heart too

lost my spark before
don't wanna take a chance with you
just to lose myself again
in the end

k
i been trying to feel okay
losing pieces of myself everyday
she is gone
i can't relate
love is dead
i'm insane
delusions in my head
nowhere to escape
consumed by thoughts
i'm not what she wants
sleeping just to feel okay
broken ever since she texted "k"
is that all you could say?
i guess this is moving on now
deleting all your pictures on my phone now
becoming the man
i was supposed to be
before i met you
seek out my dreams
and leave this town
i don't wanna stay
that day
i didn't even know what to say
k
is that all you could say?
time to go our separate ways now...
i love myself now...

akhira

you are perfect to me
when you lose hope
you will always have a home
in me

softie

and the love within you
is gonna grow again
gonna hope again
don't let go
just yet
pain is the beginning of progress
stuck
in the process
of loving again
i got wrong it before
long before
i lose control
when i fall
that weekend
i was in my head
going
through emotions
you put me through
in the end
we became
strangers again
it's strange how it ends
with feelings lost
and i'm in love
with someone i used to know
things will never be like before

cloud

trying to make up for the pain
i caused in august

i know what's inside of me
is never enough
i only saw what i wanted
now i'm up all night on IG

trying to figure out
why you blocked me

now what i love
is all lost

you don't call me back
you know i'm not okay

i want to text you
just to remind you
that i'm still here

but then i remember
you know i'm here
you just don't care

akhira

no, the moon

the moon is always shining somewhere
i just gotta get there

can't count how many times
i left
just to come back
realizing i could never quit

what saved me
you saved me

now i'm losing myself again
writing with cold hands

you don't understand
you don't understand

i can't take back what i said
and the haste decisions i made
when i was upset
afraid that this would be the end

eden

heaven, i don't deserve
chose eden on earth

hell after death
was it really worth?
a life with no remorse
regret with no tears in my eyes

i was lost in this world

chasing pleasures
to cure my pain

this dunya will never be worth it in the end

Made in the USA
Middletown, DE
31 August 2024

60130052R00086